THEN AND THERE SERIES
GENERAL EDITOR
MARJORIE REEVES

C000263840

Merthyr Iron and Merthyr Riots 1750–1860

EVAN DAVIES

Illustrated from contemporary sources

LONGMAN

LONGMAN GROUP UK LIMITED
Longman House, Burnt Mill, Harlow, Essex CM20 2 JE, England
and Associated Companies throughout the World

First published 1987

ISBN 0 582 22330 X

Set in 11/12½ Baskerville, Linotron 202
Produced by Longman Group (F.E.) Ltd
Printed in Hong Kong

Acknowledgements

We are indebted to the author, Elizabeth Davies, and Stewart Williams Publishers for permission to reproduce slightly adapted extracts from 'Life in a Nineteenth–Century Iron Town' in *Glamorgan Historian* Vol. 12.

Small extracts taken from: R. M. Evans, *Children in the Mines*, National Museum of Wales 1972, pages 26, 27; R. M. Evans, *Children in the Iron Industry*, National Museum of Wales 1978, pages 25, 29; E. A. Davies, 'Life in a Nineteenth-Century Iron Town', *Stewart Williams' Glamorgan Historian* Vol. 12, pages 31, 32, 38–9; F. Vaughan, 'Poor Relief in Merthyr in the Nineteenth Century', *Merthyr Historian* Vol. 2, 1976, pages 36, 41. The sequence of events in Chapters 7–9 is drawn from: Gwyn Williams, *The Merthyr Rising*, Croom Helm 1978.

We are grateful to the following for permission to reproduce photographs: Aerofilms Limited, page 21; BBC Hulton Picture Library, page 26; British Library, page 34; The Central Library, Merthyr Tydfil, page 40; Jeremy Lowe of the Welsh School of Architecture, UWIST Cardiff, page 38; Mansell Collection, pages 7, 8, 12, 24, 27, 28, 52; National Library of Wales, page 48; Science Museum, London, page 13; Welsh Industrial and Maritime Museum, pages 16, 43. Cover: Riots at Merthyr Tydfil, 1831. Rioters bathing their standard bearer's hands in blood. Mansell Collection.

Contents

To the reader

In 1874 a Welsh minister on a visit to Pennsylvania in the USA was called to the deathbed of a Welsh ironworker called Ieuan Parker. The dying man had emigrated to America from South Wales many years before and now wanted to make his last confession.

Ieuan Parker had left Merthyr Tydfil, with many more Welsh workers, because he did not want to starve. Because they were ironworkers they came to the great ironworks of Pennsylvania and settled down there.

But Parker was escaping from something else besides starvation. On that night in 1874 he told his story – how in 1831, over forty years before, he had taken part in a workers' rebellion in the town of Merthyr. He told of how he had stabbed a Highland soldier in the leg, thus committing a crime for which in those days the punishment was death. What Ieuan Parker really wanted to confess was that he had let another man be hanged for his crime. This other man was the famous Dic Penderyn, who had died on the gallows so many years before.

Perhaps Ieuan Parker died a happy man, now that he had confessed his crime. Perhaps his confession was the result of his own imagination. In any case, nothing could be done so long after the crime. The people of Merthyr knew all along that Dic Penderyn was not really a guilty man.

This book tells the story of Merthyr's iron industry and how people lived and worked in Merthyr. It also tells the tale of one of Merthyr's most exciting happenings, the rising of 1831, when the workers rose up against their masters. It was one of the most serious rebellions in Britain's modern history.

1 The beginnings of the Merthyr iron industry

Imagine that we are walking beside the River Taff in a beautiful valley in about 1750. It is a quiet, lonely valley. All around us are rocky hills, grazing sheep and rushing mountain streams flowing into the river. Very few people live here. There are no towns in the valley and only a few villages. One of these villages is called Merthyr Tydfil, high up in the valley towards the high mountains where the river started. Merthyr is a sleepy little place of only four hundred people. We would never imagine that this lonely valley would soon become a bustling, busy place and that Merthyr would be the largest town in Wales where a great deal of the world's iron would be made.

IRON MAKING

How did this happen? The secret lay in those hills and streams. In the hills was a great deal of ironstone, which is rock containing bits of iron. There was plenty of limestone too. Some of the hills were covered in trees, whose wood could be slowly smouldered to make *charcoal*. Iron was made by mixing ironstone, limestone and charcoal together in a furnace, heating it for several hours and blowing blasts of air through it with bellows. This made it very hot indeed. Then the furnace men pulled out the plug in the furnace and let the molten (liquid) iron run into a channel they had made in the sandy floor. This was shaped like a sow feeding her piglets so this kind of iron, when it had cooled and hardened was called *pig iron*. Look over the page to see how it was done.

But pig iron was still full of bits which were not pure iron (*impurities*), so it had to be heated again to get rid of more of 5

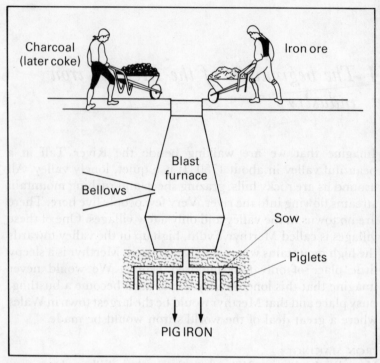

Charcoal (later coke)

Iron ore

Bellows

Blast furnace

Sow

Piglets

PIG IRON

these. Then it was run into more sandy moulds. This kind of iron was called *cast iron*, which was purer than pig iron but which broke easily if knocked. You could make an even purer and stronger sort of iron by reheating the bars and hammering them with a very strong hammer worked by water power. This was *wrought iron*.

Workers in south Wales had been making iron like this for 200 years or more. People needed small amounts of iron for tools and simple machines and got what they wanted from small furnaces scattered all over the countryside. But in the middle of the eighteenth century people all over the world began to need more iron. This was partly because there were more people and partly because they were inventing newer and bigger machines for making all sorts of things in the new factories that were being built. When something is badly

Making wrought iron with a water-powered hammer

needed people usually find ways of getting more of it more quickly. So in South Wales men started to mine more ironstone and build more furnaces.

Two things helped them to make more iron and to make it more quickly. First, they found they could melt it more quickly by using coke, made from coal, instead of charcoal. This was the invention of Abraham Darby of Coalbrookdale. Secondly, fast-rushing streams provided water power to drive machines and hammers. Merthyr's hills had plenty of coal and fast-flowing streams.

THE START OF MERTHYR'S IRONWORKS
Clever businessmen from England came to South Wales to start up new ironworks. They saw the chance to make a lot of money by selling iron all over the world. They needed capital, 7

that is large amounts of money to spend on new furnaces and on the machinery which would be needed before they could make any profit. In England there were rich merchants and landowners with money to spare, which they lent to the new *ironmasters*. The ironmasters also needed workers and they found these easily in South Wales because there were too many farm workers earning very small wages. These workers trooped into the new ironworks where they could earn more money, although still too little. High up in the valleys of Glamorgan and Monmouthshire (Gwent), on the edge of the coalfields, the new ironmasters quickly turned villages into towns. New furnaces started up and workers' houses were built. That was how iron towns like Aberdare, Blaenavon, Nantyglo and, above all, Merthyr Tydfil, grew.

Actually the very first ironmaster in Merthyr was a Welshman, Thomas Lewis of Llanishen. He started a furnace at Dowlais, a short distance from Merthyr village in 1748 with money lent by Bristol merchants. In 1767 he made John Guest, a Staffordshire man, the manager of Dowlais iron works, and gradually Guest became the main owner of the business. He was a good businessman and by 1806 he had three furnaces producing 5000 tons of iron a year.

Around the old village of Merthyr four huge ironworks grew

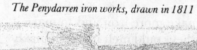

The Penydarren iron works, drawn in 1811

up. Each one had its own furnaces, warehouses, machine sheds and worker's cottages. Dowlais was the first. In 1765 a rich London merchant, Anthony Bacon, started the second at Plymouth, and at the same time began to build a furnace at Cyfarthfa. Bacon soon appointed Richard Hill to manage the Plymouth iron works, which was the smallest works and produced specially good iron. At Cyfarthfa Richard Crawshay became manager. As a Yorkshire boy he had run away from home and done well in business because he was a pushing sort of person. As you might expect, he soon made Cyfarthfa the largest ironworks in the world, with six furnaces producing 11,000 tons in 1806.

The fourth ironworks, Penydarren, was started in 1784 by two brothers from Staffordshire, Samuel and Jeremiah Homfray, and a London merchant, George Forman. These three brought Yorkshire miners with them, who were unpopular at first and got into fights with the Welsh workers, especially on Saturday nights. By 1806 Penydarren was making 3000 tons of iron a year in its three furnaces. Look at the map on page 45 to see the four ironworks round Merthyr village.

INVENTIONS IN THE IRON INDUSTRY

What made the ironmasters so successful? One reason was that they were bold enough to use new inventions and to spend a lot of money on improvements. So in Merthyr, soon after 1760, they began to use a *blast engine* invented by a man called James Smeaton. It blew air through the furnace, heating it up more quickly. This did away with the bellows worked by hand.

In 1784 an important new way of making iron called *puddling* and rolling was found. Samuel Cort of Portsmouth got credit as the inventor, but a Merthyr foreman called Peter Onions was already using this method. Richard Crawshay was the first to spot its value and it became known as the 'Welsh method'. It worked like this. Men called puddlers reheated pig iron in a small furnace, stirring it with long tongs while the impurities were burned out. After puddling, lumps of half-melted iron were rolled and rerolled between rollers to squeeze out even 9 more impurities. This method was much quicker than the old way of hammering with huge hammers. Crawshay and the other ironmasters could produce much more and much better wrought iron more quickly.

Finally, in the 1780s and 1790s, they began to use steam engines made by the great Birmingham engineers, Matthew Boulton and James Watt, instead of water power. Water power had been better than hand power or horse power but it was useless if water was short. Steam power was much stronger and always available, so the ironmasters began to drive their new rolling machines by steam.

CHANGES IN TRANSPORT

The ironmasters soon had to do something about transport. Their iron bars were being carried down to Cardiff on the coast by mules because the tracks were too rough for anything else. This was far too slow. In 1769 Anthony Bacon improved the road so that carts could be used, but this did not satisfy the ironmasters either. Between 1790 and 1794 Richard Crawshay spent a huge sum of money making the Glamorgan Canal from Merthyr to Cardiff. It was twenty-five miles long with fifty *locks* to carry its loads through the hilly country. Once finished, it could carry the iron down to Cardiff much more cheaply and quickly. The canal is on the map inside the front cover. The ironmasters also built railroads, that is iron rails along which mules could pull trucks of coal, ironstone or iron. They used these between the mines, the ironworks and the canal.

One day Richard Crawshay bet Samuel Homfray a thousand pounds that no-one could invent a moving steam engine to pull the trucks instead of mules. Homfray got hold of a very clever engineer from Cornwall, Richard Trevithick, and finally won his bet. In February 1804 the first railway engine ran along the railroad from Penydarren to the canal at Abercynon. Its proud inventor walked beside it with a spanner in his hand. On this first journey the tall chimney was knocked off by a low bridge. Trevithick had to use his spanner to put the chimney back again!

2 Merthyr at its greatest – the nineteenth century

In 1800 Merthyr was the largest iron town in Wales and Cyfarthfa was the largest single ironworks in the whole world. For another seventy years Merthyr was to remain one of the world's most important iron centres. Its iron industry in 1850 was making sixteen times as much iron as it had made in 1806. The town's population had grown from 8000 to 50,000 in the same period.

Why did Merthyr grow so fast? In many parts of the world, especially in Britain, more and more industries were being started. These new industries needed machines, and machines were made of iron. Iron was being used more and more for all sorts of other things too – iron bedsteads, iron bridges, iron ships, even iron buildings, like the famous Crystal Palace exhibition hall in London. But more than anything else iron was being used for the new railways. Of course the engines themselves were made of iron, and so were many of the carriages and the seats, but most of the iron was used in the rails. Thousands and thousands of miles of rail tracks were being built all over the world after the 1820s. In 1825 the rails for the world's first proper railway, the Stockton to Darlington Railway in the North of England, were made at Dowlais. After that rails became Merthyr's most important product for many years to come. Dowlais was famous for its good quality rails and visitors came from all over the world to see them being made.

INVENTIONS AND IMPROVEMENTS

Better and quicker ways of making iron were another reason why the Merthyr iron industry grew so fast. The Merthyr iron-   11

How Merthyr iron was used: the Crumlin Viaduct, made from iron, was 500 metres long

masters, especially the Guests and the Crawshays, had the good sense and the large amounts of money needed to use these new inventions. In doing so they produced more iron and made more profits.

One great improvement was the *hot blast*. This was the idea of James Neilson of Glasgow in 1828. Up to then cold air had been blown into the furnace to make the fire burn hotter. Now the ironmakers blasted very hot air into the furnace. This was so hot that it heated up the furnace much more quickly. Because it burned away the impurities very quickly, the furnace could now use raw coal instead of coke. In addition it used much less coal than before. Instead of taking eight tons of coal to make one ton of iron only five tons were needed.

Then, in 1839, came James Naysmith's invention of the steam hammer. This was a gigantic hammer worked by steam power. It beat the impurities out of immense bars of iron much more quickly than the older, smaller hammers and rollers. The earth shook with its hammer-beats and the air roared with its mighty noise.

Next came the two most important inventions of all. They

were important because they made it possible to make *steel* cheaply and quickly. Steel is a very pure type of iron with carbon added. Up to the 1850s it was slow and difficult to make and very expensive to buy. However people preferred it to iron because it was stronger and did not break so easily.

In 1856 Henry Bessemer invented the Bessemer converter. This was a small furnace which looked rather like a concrete mixer. When it had been filled with liquid pig iron, a hot blast of air was blown through it. The temperature became much hotter than in a full-size blast furnace. The heat made vast numbers of bright, spitting sparks shoot out of the top of the furnace as the impurities were burned very quickly away. The converter took only about half an hour to turn pig iron into steel. The liquid steel was then tipped into moulds. The Dowlais ironworks was the first in the world to experiment with Bessemer's invention. Soon much steel was being made in Merthyr, as well as iron.

A few years later, in 1866, a new method of making steel was

Bessemer converters at work at Ebbw Vale in the 1860s

invented by a man called William Siemens. It became known as the Siemens-Martin method. Instead of using a converter, this method used a furnace filled with a mixture of melted pig iron and bits of scrap iron. Hot air and gases were burned over the iron to heat it to a very high temperature and to burn out the impurities. This method took longer than the Bessemer converter but it produced larger amounts of steel and made use of scrap iron. Later on, ironworks used it instead of the Bessemer converter.

MERTHYR'S OTHER INDUSTRIES — COAL AND TRANSPORT

The ironmasters of Merthyr were interested not only in the iron industry. They could not afford to be. Coal to make the iron, and transport to carry it away were very important to them. It took at least five tons of coal to make one ton of iron, so you can see that the iron masters needed every ton of coal they could get. Fortunately Merthyr was very rich in coal so the ironmasters were able to start new coalmines near the town. At first the coal was dug straight out of the ground or out of *adits*, tunnels going into the hillside. Later on more and more deep pits had to be dug to get at the coal. These cost a lot of money but the ironmasters had to spend it. Without large amounts of coal the ironworks could not make iron. The ironmasters employed nearly as many coalminers as ironworkers. Other mineowners opened pits too, not to provide coal for the ironworks but to sell it all over the country. Merthyr coal was popular because it was not too smoky. One of the most famous of these coal owners was a woman named Lucy Thomas who took over her husband's mine when he died and made a fortune out of it. She was one of the very few women to make a success in business in those days.

Soon the ironmasters saw that the Glamorgan Canal could not carry all the iron and coal being sent out of Merthyr. They were making the rails for railways in other places, and they could see that what Merthyr needed was a railway herself. In 1834 the ironmasters Guest and Hill set up a railway company to build a line called the Taff Vale Railway. It was to run from Merthyr down to the new docks which were being built in Cardiff to export the coal and iron. The new company invited the most famous engineer in the kingdom to be in charge of the railway. His name was Isambard Kingdom Brunel. Only the best would do for the Merthyr ironmasters. Brunel made a good job of the Taff Vale Railway. For most of the way the railway followed the line of the canal. The countryside was so hilly in one place that the railway engines could not carry their loads up the steep slope. At the top of the hill Brunel had to build a very powerful steam engine which pulled the trains up the hill on a moving chain. This lasted until stronger railway engines were invented. In 1841 the railway finally reached Merthyr and there were great celebrations as the first load of iron went down the valley to Cardiff.

MERTHYR AT ITS GREATEST

With all these happenings and changes in the iron, coal and transport industries, you can see how Merthyr became the largest town in Wales. By 1860 it had over 50,000 people. By this time iron had been made in Merthyr for over a century. The amount of iron being made increased from 16,000 tons in 1806 to nearly 300,000 tons in 1850. All four ironworks had grown large, especially Dowlais under the Guests and Cyfarthfa under the Crawshays. In the 1840s Dowlais overtook Cyfarthfa as the largest ironworks in Merthyr and in the world. In 1870 it produced nearly 200,000 tons of iron and steel and employed 9000 people. 5000 of them worked in the ironworks and 4000 in the Guest mines.

Yet Merthyr's importance was coming to an end. People now wanted steel, not iron, and Merthyr was not really suited to the new steel industry. Its ironstone was running out and was not of exactly the right sort for making steel. Special foreign ironstone had to be imported, and for this it was more convenient to build steelworks on the coast instead of high up in the valley at Merthyr. Plymouth and Penydarren ironworks never made steel and soon had to close down. Dowlais did continue to make large amounts of steel for many years to come. After a long shut- 15

A painting of the Dowlais ironworks at its height in 1840

down Cyfarthfa too went over to steel making. But iron and steel were no longer Merthyr's main industry. Instead coal became more important. By the 1860s Merthyr's great days of iron-making were over, but for over a hundred years it had been the world's greatest iron town.

3 The ironmasters

The most important people in Merthyr during its great days as an iron town were the ironmasters. The Crawshays of Cyfarthfa, the Guests of Dowlais, the Hills of Plymouth and the Homfrays of Penydarren had great power over their workers. Most Merthyr people worked for them. In the middle of the nineteenth century even the smallest ironworks, Penydarren, employed over 2000 people, while the largest, Dowlais, employed 9000. These were enormous numbers of workers for those days.

The ironmasters had power and wealth outside Merthyr too, especially the Crawshays and the Guests. They owned the canal and the railway that took the iron from Merthyr to its customers all over the world. The Crawshays owned several ironworks and mines in other parts of South Wales, as well as a large and successful merchant company in London. The Guests too had iron mines and large estates in other parts of England and Wales. In addition, Sir Josiah John Guest, the greatest ironmaster of all, found the time to be Merthyr's MP. It is no wonder that these men were able to leave millions of pounds at their deaths; they were some of the richest people in the whole country.

Yet it was in Merthyr that their real interests lay. For about a hundred years, three or four generations of ironmaster families ruled the town. In fact the Crawshays were called the 'iron kings'.

What sort of men were these ironmasters? More than anything else they were excellent businessmen. They knew how to make money by running their works efficiently and selling their iron at the greatest profit. They realised the value of building roads, canals and railways and the need to use new inventions. They appointed the best managers and the best engineers like Richard Trevithick. They were very energetic men, hard at work for long hours, giving orders and seeing to every detail. Even though they had all the power they did not look down on their workmen. Their grand homes were all built very close to the works so that they could keep an eye on things. They could often do the worker' jobs themselves because they had spent all their lives near the works. Instead of sending their sons away to expensive boarding schools, they set them to work at an early age, learning the business of making iron and creating profits. But although they were all good businessmen, the ironmasters were very different sorts of people, as you can see by looking at the two greatest families, the Crawshays and the Guests.

THE CRAWSHAYS

Richard Crawshay, who first bought Cyfarthfa, was a very strong-minded man. As a young boy he quarrelled with his father and ran away from home. He was quick-tempered, always arguing with his sons and his workers. Yet he would often apologise for losing his temper and he was a popular employer. He was not popular with his son William, however, whom he treated very harshly. William was a proud and violent man who quarrelled with his father so much that he came to hate Merthyr.

When William, known as William Crawshay I, inherited Cyfarthfa in 1809, he decided to run the London side of the family business. He left his son, William Crawshay II, to run the ironworks. As before, father and son quarrelled bitterly because William II wanted to own the works as well as to run them. Both Williams were cunning and clever businessmen, but it was William II who for nearly forty years ran the largest ironworks in the world.

William II loved Cyfarthfa. He was a peculiar mixture of a man. On the hillside overlooking the furnaces he built a huge new castle as his home. He did this to show off his wealth and his pride. Yet when he was asked by the King to become a nobleman, he turned the chance down. He paid his workers better wages than the other ironmasters, but he made them work very hard and do exactly as they were told. He knew many of his workers by name and learned Welsh so that he could talk to them. He would go drinking with them in the public houses, but he could also be a very hard master indeed. When the workers of Merthyr rioted in 1831 he was bitterly blamed for the shootings that happened. (You can read about these riots in the last three chapters of this book.) When he died he was not a popular man.

Robert Crawshay, William II's son, was only twenty-two when he became ironmaster. He too was a good businessman and like his father was both loved and hated by his workforce. At first he treated his workers very well and would always listen to their complaints. He was so popular that when he got married his workers unharnessed the horses from his coach and pulled it along themselves. He kept Cyfarthfa going in the 1860s for his workers' sake even though by this time he was losing money. Yet he changed after a serious illness which left him deaf and almost blind. He became unpleasant and cruel towards his family and his workers. When his employees started a trade union to get better wages, he was so offended that he closed down the works for over five years. On his gravestone he ordered these simple words to be carved – 'God forgive me'. He was the last of the great Crawshay ironmasters. Like the others he always liked to get his own way.

THE GUESTS
The Guest family was steadier than the Crawshays. The first two Guests, John and Thomas were serious men and good ironmasters, but it was Josiah John Guest who was the real business genius of the Guest family. He ran the Dowlais works for forty-five years, taking over in 1807 at the age of twenty-two. It was he who made Dowlais overtake Cyfarthfa and become the largest ironworks in the world. Josiah John Guest was

always the first to use new inventions, the first to make railway rails in large quantities, the first to see the need for a railway line between Merthyr and Cardiff. He was an inventor too and helped to make the first steam hooter. He was such an energetic man that he could find time for many other things. He became Merthyr's MP in 1832 and spent a lot of time and money on local matters. He set up churches, chapels, schools, clubs and libraries in Merthyr. For all these activities he was rewarded with the title Sir Josiah John Guest by Queen Victoria. He knew his workers well and was liked and respected by most of them. He was a steady man, not up-and-down like the Crawshays. Even so, he kept his workers firmly in their place, paid low wages and stamped out strikes. He did not worry about the terrible poverty in which his workers lived. He was always the master.

Sir Josiah John's wife, Lady Charlotte Guest, was a very unusual woman. She came from a rich and noble family and married Sir Josiah John when she was only twenty-one and he was forty-eight. She nicknamed her husband 'Merthyr'. As soon as she arrived at Dowlais she began to take an interest in the ironworks and became a great help to her husband. She was more interested than he was in looking after the workers, especially caring for their children's education and health. Lady Charlotte learned Welsh and translated the famous book of Welsh legends, the 'Mabinogion'. She also found time to bring up ten children of her own. When Sir Josiah John died in 1852 Lady Charlotte ran the business very successfully for several years.

THE HOMES OF THE IRONMASTERS

The differences between the ironmasters and their workers were very plain to see. The ironmasters were among the richest people in the land and their workers were among the poorest. This showed in their houses. At first they lived in fairly ordinary homes, but as they grew wealthier they began to show off their wealth with grand houses. The Homfrays built a fine mansion at Penydarren and Sir Josiah John Guest had one a

Dowlais. The grandest and most expensive of all was Cyfarthfa Castle. It was the largest building in Merthyr, with its 15 towers, 72 rooms and 365 windows. It had specially heated greenhouses for growing rare fruits such as pineapples, grapes and peaches. When William Crawshay II was choosing the carpet, he was offended by the salesman who showed him a cheap one. He insisted on seeing the very best quality and must have enjoyed seeing the man's surprised face when he gave his order: 'A quarter of a mile of your best carpet, please, for my new castle'.

The people in these magnificent houses lived very differently from the poor workers. At Cyfarthfa Castle and Dowlais House important visitors were entertained, even kings and princes.

A modern photograph of Cyfartha Castle

There were parties, and dinners with twenty courses. Sometimes even Cyfarthfa Castle was not big enough for a ball or a banquet and William Crawshay would turn his wagon shed at great cost into a splendid ballroom.

THE POWER OF THE IRONMASTERS

We can easily see how the ironmasters were able to rule over Merthyr. There were not many places to work at except the ironworks and mines. The four ironmasters would usually agree to keep wages low. Whenever there was trouble, they would band together to stamp out strikes and riots. They would all refuse to employ known troublemakers. They owned most of the houses that their workpeople lived in. They often owned the shops where they forced their workers to buy their goods. They built the schools, churches and chapels which their workpeople attended. The ironmasters were very powerful men indeed. They had many ways of keeping control over their workers but the greatest of these was at work. There they had complete power.

4 Working for the ironmasters

People came to Merthyr to find work. In those days there was not enough work for everyone on the farms, while the ironworks needed more workers. So people were glad to find work in Merthyr. Wages there were higher than on the farms, although the work was very hard. Workers crowded into the little town and learned new jobs in the ironworks and the mines.

Dic Penderyn was one of these workers. His real name was Richard Lewis and he was born at a cottage called Penderyn near Aberafon in 1808. As a child he walked thirty-five miles with his family to find work in Merthyr. In his boyhood and youth Dic worked at several of the jobs in the iron industry.

Men, women and children worked for the ironmasters. They did not all work in the ironworks. Over half of them worked in the coal pits and ironstone mines or did jobs like labouring, carrying things or looking after the horses. The vast stables at Dowlais contained over 500 horses which must have required many men to look after them.

Inside the ironworks the furnaces had to be kept going all the time. If ever one cooled down, it took weeks to get it going again. It could not stop for the night, for the weekend or for a holiday. The working day was divided into two shifts of twelve hours each. The workers worked one week of night shift, then one week of day shift. Six o'clock was the time to start and finish work. Exactly at six the Dowlais steam hooter, which Sir Josiah John himself helped to invent, whistled noisily. It could be heard for miles around. Sternly it commanded people to get out of bed, or to go wearily home. Some people worked for seven days a week, the lucky ones for six. Holidays were almost unknown, but sometimes the ironmasters would grant a day off, keeping the furnaces alight of course. They were hard masters. If a worker came late he was fined; if he was absent from work, he could be dismissed.

At work the employees were organised into teams. In charge of each team was a skilled man known as an *overman* or a *contractor*. He gave the orders to his team. Very often some of these would be his own children. Workers were not paid separately. Instead the overman received a single amount which he would then share out among his team. This usually happened in a public house and an unfair overman would try to cheat his team out of their hard-earned wages. To make matters even worse many of the ironworkers were paid only once a month, which meant that they often got into debt towards the end of the month. This way of paying was known as long pay.

In those days there were hardly any laws forcing employers to make their works safe and healthy. Ironworks, with all their hot metal and clanging machinery, were very dangerous places

An accident like this, in a Merthyr colliery in the 1860s, happened only too often

A perilous passage

indeed to work in. So were the coal and ironstone mines. Terrible accidents were happening all the time. If a worker was injured the employer said it was his own fault. The ironmasters paid no *compensation*, and the injured worker would very often lose his job. Even if a worker avoided accidents, earning a living was tiring and dangerous. Work was very, very hard indeed.

WORKING IN THE COAL AND IRONSTONE MINES

Many workers in Merthyr were ironstone miners. The hillsides round Merthyr were full of ironstone mines. At first the ironstone was dug straight out of the ground, but as time went by the miners had to go down into deeper pits to get the ironstone out. The hillsides were divided into 'patches', each one under the orders of a contractor. As the contractor was paid for the amount he sent to the ironworks, he and his team had to work very fast. Eight tons of useless stone had to be pick-axed and shovelled to get just one ton of ironstone. Then the ironstone had to be cleaned by damming a stream and washing away the soil. An eighty-year old woman described how she did this job in 1840. 'I work here cleaning the iron ore. I have two girls to help me and we start at eight o'clock and finish at six o'clock.' How bitterly cold it must have been up on that dark, wet mountainside at eight o'clock on a winter's morning. Yet the work could not stop. The hungry blast furnaces had to be fed every day with tons and tons of ironstone.

Coal too had to be mined. In the coalpits the work was backbreaking and long. Men had to pickaxe the coal out of the solid rock. They often had to do this kneeling or even lying down because the layers of coal were often so narrow. Their mouths, nostrils and lungs were always full of coal dust and the air was so hot and stuffy that they worked without clothes. Women and older children loaded the coal into tubs or baskets and carried it away. As you can see from the picture on page 27 they were often chained to the tubs and had to crawl along on their hands and knees. They even had to climb all the way to the surface with heavy loads of coal on their backs. Even very young children were employed in the mines. A six-year old girl called Mary 25

Ironstone mines were hard places to work in. What dangers were there in this mine drawn in 1820?

Davies worked in ironmaster Hill's mines. It was her job to sit in the darkness and open the underground doors for loads of coal to pass through. A government inspector found her asleep when he visited the mine in 1840. She told him, 'I went to sleep because my lamp had gone out. I was frightened because someone had stolen my bread and cheese, I think it was the rats.'

Even worse than the hardness of the work underground were the terrible dangers. Sometimes miners drowned in underground floods or were buried under tons of rocks when the roof caved in. Worst of all were the explosions of poisonous gas and dust. They would blast violently through the narrow tunnels, killing or injuring anyone in their way. Phillip Phillips, a nine-year old lad, stated to the inspector, 'I started work when I was seven. I get very tired sitting in the dark by the door so I go to

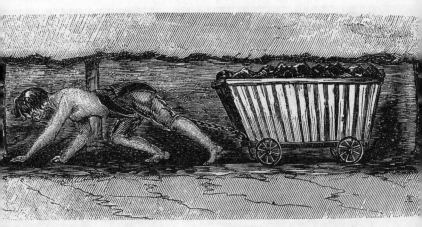

A child at work in a mine, as shown in a report by Parliamentary Commissioners in 1842

sleep. Nearly a year ago there was an accident and most of us were burned. I was carried home by a man. It hurt very much because all the skin was burnt off my face. I couldn't work for six months.' Phillip was lucky. Many others were torn apart by explosions. It was stories like this that led to a law being passed in 1842. This law prevented mineowners from employing any women and girls at all and any boys under ten in the coal mines. Even so, this law did not apply to iron mines and did nothing to improve the dreadful hardships underground.

INSIDE THE IRONWORKS

Once the coal and ironstone reached the ironworks other workers took over. Each big blast furnace had its team of 'chargers' who filled the furnace at the top with ironstone, coal and limestone. The flames roared upwards singeing their faces as they tipped in their loads. Down below, more highly-skilled workers and their teams were in charge. The *founders* were the men who let the liquid iron out of the furnace and into the moulds. Then the iron went into the smaller puddling furnaces. Each one of these was under the command of a 'first-rate' puddler, a very skilled man. He gave the orders to the other 27

Puddlers at work – taking a ball of white hot metal from a puddling furnace

puddlers and to the firemen who threw fuel into the white-hot furnaces. 'Pull-up' boys and girls had the job of lifting the furnace door and pulling the heavy balls of iron across the floor.

As you can imagine, all those who worked with the iron had very uncomfortable lives. The *foundry* was so hot that puddlers drank gallons of beer every day. They did not get drunk because they sweated all the beer away. The glare of the furnace was so bright that it weakened the eyes of those who looked into it too often. It could even blind them. The greatest danger of all was a 'blow-out', when flames leapt out of the furnace door or even burst through the furnace wall, spitting out melted iron. Many terrible deaths and injuries were caused in this way. Two brothers aged nine and thirteen stated, 'Our father is a puddler and our brother works with him. Our time is from six to six and we get very tired by the end. We get burned a little now and then. We have never been to school so we cannot read.'

The hot metal was still a danger after it left the furnaces. It still had to be hammered or rolled into shape. The workers had to watch out because the hot iron was pulled rapidly across the floor. Men and boys as 'shinglers' caught it with tongs as it passed from one side of the roller to the other. The machines had no safety guards so a hand or an arm could easily be crushed between the hot rollers. Morgan Lewis, a nine-year old boy working at Plymouth Ironworks said, 'I have been working here for two years. I used to work at the squeezing machine, straightening bars of iron. The work is very hard and I get tired, but my dinner gives me strength for I share my father's meat. Sometimes I get burned at the furnace.'

As the iron was being made lots of waste material was left behind, known as *slag*. While this was still red-hot it was loaded into wagons by young girls. It was the job of these 'tip girls' to push the wagons to the top of the huge slag heaps, which were forever growing like ugly mountains over Merthyr.

A child born in Merthyr could expect a lifetime doing jobs like these. Even if he escaped death or injury, he could only expect long hours of uncomfortable and very hard toil.

5 Making ends meet

The only really rich people in Merthyr were the ironmaster families. After them came the middle classes of the town, just a few hundred people. These were the doctors, the managers, the lawyers and mostly the shopkeepers of the town. Below them were the workers and their families, thousands and thousands of people mainly employed in the ironworks and the mines.

WAGES

Most of the workers were very poor indeed. In 1849 a reporter visited Merthyr and made a list of weekly wages:

Job	Wage				
	£	s.	d.	(£	p)
Roller	1	5	0	1	25
Founder	1	3	0	1	15
First-rate puddler	1	0	0	1	0
Assistant puddler		15	0		75
Furnace-filler		14	0		70
Ironstone and coal miners		12/15	0		60/75
Coal loaders, labourers etc		10	0		50
Pull-up children, tip girls etc		3/7	0		15/35

As you can imagine, the workers complained bitterly to the reporter that their money was not enough. They said that they had just been told by the ironmasters that as much as 1s. 6d. or 2s. (7½p or 10p) was to be taken off their wages. One of the big problems in the iron industry was that sometimes the ironmasters could not sell their iron at high prices. When this happened the easiest thing they could do was to reduce wages. 1848 was a bad year for wages. Some of the more skilled workers said that a few years earlier they had been earning twice as much.

What could these wages buy? A miner earning 12s. (60p) a week, with a wife and five children, probably spent his money like this:

	s.	d.	(p)
House rent	2	3	11
Doctor's fund at work		1½	½
Candles for work		10	4
Charges paid to foreman		3½	1½
Beer money at work		6	2½
Butter (½lb/226g)		4½	2
Flour (28lb/12.7kg)	3	4½	17
Cheese (3½lb/1.6kg)	2	0	10
Tea (¼lb/113g)	1	0	5
Sugar (1 lb/453g)		4½	2
Meat (1lb/453g)		4½	2
Potatoes (2lb/907g)		1½	½
Yeast, use of baker's oven		4½	2
	12	0	60

The miner also received free coal on top of his 12s. Even so, it is clear that 12s. was not enough to feed a family of two adults and five children. The miner told the reporter that he could only afford meat once a week. In those days it was usual for the man of the house to have the greatest share of food, especially of the cheese and meat. This would keep up his strength for work. After all, if he fell sick and lost his job, the whole family would suffer.

Have you noticed what is not on the list? There is no milk for the children, no vegetables to provide vitamins, no eggs, no nice cakes and puddings, no clothes, no shoes and, of course, no money at all for treats or presents. It is not surprising that the miner was glad to send out his children to work as soon as they were old enough – even if he had to take his child down the pit to sit in the dark all day. The pay of two or three working children made all the difference, even though they earned so little.

Remember that most of the workers were paid 10s. (50p) or under. Only a few skilled workers earned £1 or over. They of course would have more meat and cheese and more 'luxuries', but one puddler admitted to the reporter, 'Though I am better off than hundreds, I can hardly live'. The poor labourers were much worse off. One of them, who had a wife and five children, reported, 'During the two years I have been here I have not used one pound (453g) of butter or cheese altogether. I try to give my family a little meat on Sunday, some cow's cheek or like that.' It is sad to wonder what happened to the family of the miner who stated to the reporter, 'I have a wife and six children. I have not had enough bread and neither has my family for a year although I am in full work. Scores of times I have stayed in the public house where I was paid till I had spent one half of my money, as do a great number of men.' It is not surprising that working men drank so much, that their wives soon lost their youth and beauty and that their children died so easily.

TRUCK SHOPS

One thing that the workers hated so much for keeping them poor was the *truck shop*. Truck shops were special shops owned by the ironmasters where the workers had to buy their goods. The ironmasters made sure of this by paying their workers in tokens or tickets which they could only change at the truck shop. In the truck shop prices would often be higher than in other shops, and what was sold would be of poorer quality. Because the workers were only paid once a month many of them ran out of money before the next wages were due. The truck shop would allow them to buy on loan until the next pay day. This would happen month after month, keeping the worker always in debt to the ironmaster's shop.

A token paid to Penydarren workers for exchange in the truck shop

Not all the ironmasters had truck shops. The Guests set one up at Dowlais in 1796, and the Homfrays had one at Penydarren. However the Crawshays and the Hills believed that truck shops were unfair and criticised the other ironmasters for having too much power over their workers. All over the country people demanded the ending of truck shops run by employers. In 1831 Parliament finally made it illegal to pay wages in anything but real money. When this happened the ironmasters closed down their truckshops.

Inside a miner's home in Gas Row, Dowlais, in the mid-nineteenth century

GETTING INTO DEBT

It was always easy to get into debt in Merthyr, especially when wages were cut. Not only the truck shops but even the ordinary shops let people get into debt by giving them goods to be paid for later. Thousands of workers would get into debt in this way, especially the lower-paid. Even though the sums of money were small they would soon mount up. Sooner or later the shopkeepers would want their money back. To do this they asked a special court called the *Court of Requests* to collect their debts for them. This court was set up in Merthyr in 1809 and it had the right to send its officials, the *bailiffs*, to collect the debt. If the workers did not have the money, the bailiffs had the right to take their possessions instead. The court then sold the seized possessions to the highest bidder and the shopkeeper was paid. In this way clocks, furniture, even Bibles, were taken away. One sick, old woman had the bed taken from under her by the bailiffs and was left dying on a pile of straw. The court's president and his bailiffs were at their busiest when wages were low and debts were high. This was the very time when the people felt bitter, angry and upset. At such times the president and the bailiffs were the most hated men in Merthyr.

THE POOR LAW

The worst-off of all in Merthyr were those who could not earn their own living. This might happen to perfectly fit men. When the ironmasters could not sell their iron, they would close down whole furnaces and sack the workers. However, at least these workers had the chance to get a job when the furnaces opened again. It was much worse for the workers who had been blinded or lost their limbs at work, or for the families of workers killed at work. The poorest of all were those too old to work and orphaned children. These very poor people were known as *paupers*. There were many of them in those days.

At that time better-off people were very hard on the poor. They blamed paupers for being poor, saying they were idle or that it was God's will that they should be poor. There was a special law called the *Poor Law* to deal with these very poor people. In each area there was a group of people called the *Board of Guardians*. These were chosen by the *ratepayers*, who were the better-off people who owned their own property. In Merthyr the Guardians were the ironmasters, managers and shopkeepers. They had to collect a special sum of money, called the *poor rate*, from the ratepayers. With this money the Board of Guardians could help the poor. Actually the Board of Guardians was often very mean. Paupers received very small amounts of money each week, just enough to keep them alive. If they had any possessions, furniture or clocks, these could be taken away from them and sold. The largest number of paupers were children whose parents had died or had deserted them. These children could not look after themselves, so the Board of   35

Guardians offered 2s. 6d. (12½p) a week to anyone who would take a pauper child. No-one really wanted these children but there were some poor people who would take them simply to get 2s. 6d. They did not really care for the children and fed them only just enough to keep them alive. These children were often made to work hard or to beg on the streets. Some of them became criminals but many of them just died. The Poor Law was not kind.

In 1834 Parliament passed the New Poor Law. This was even worse than the old one. It said that the Board of Guardians should no longer give money to unemployed people. Instead it should build a special place called the *workhouse*, where the poor should live. Pauper children should live there too. Life in the workhouse should be very bad indeed so that people would not want to go there. When a family moved into the workhouse, it was split up. Men, women and children were sent to separate parts, the food was poor and the people had to do hard work like breaking stones. The Merthyr Board of Guardians never got round to building a workhouse until 1853. When they did, some of the poor refused to enter it, preferring to starve outside. The pauper children's section was very bad indeed. An inspector who visited it in 1853 reported that the children were 'dirty backward and neglected'. It is not surprising that the poor of Merthyr hated the workhouse.

It must have been frightening to be poor in Merthyr. Most people there were so badly paid that even when they had a job their life was miserable. There was always the fear of wage cuts and unemployment. An accident or a death brought terrible heartbreaks and hardships. As usual, it was the weakest who were hit worst of all – the sick, the old and the children. For people like this making ends meet was never easy and often impossible.

6 Living and dying in Merthyr

In the hundred years following the building of the ironworks Merthyr Tydfil grew very fast indeed. At first the ironworks were just outside the village, each one surrounded by its own workers' houses. Soon the ironworks joined up with the village, as more and more people came to live in Merthyr and more furnaces were built. By 1860 Merthyr was a large town of over fifty thousand inhabitants. It was a filthy, unhealthy place, and it did not have even one hospital.

Nowadays there are laws to make sure that houses are properly built and have sewers, drains and a water supply. At the time when Merthyr was growing so fast there were no laws like these. There was not even a town council in Merthyr to run the town properly, so Merthyr became an overcrowded, dirty place. It was not a pleasant town to live in.

HOUSING

Nearly half of the workers lived in houses owned by the ironmasters. Some of the ironmasters built quite good houses for their employees. Anthony Hill of Plymouth built a famous group of houses known as the Triangle, where each house had four rooms and a little front garden. But most of the workers' houses were much smaller than this.

Many houses had only two or three rooms. There were no bathrooms, of course, and no proper kitchens. All the cooking would be done on the fireplace. Very often the upper storey would be a single room with no windows where all the family slept. The best working class homes were simple rows of houses on a street, with a small yard at the back of each one. In these

One-down, two-up houses in Pond Street, Dowlais, around 1840

houses the better-off workers lived. You can see from the picture how narrow and small they are.

Not all houses were built in streets in those days. It was cheaper to build them in a square with a large yard in the middle. This was entered by one narrow alleyway between two of the houses. The yard was shared by all the inhabitants and had a shared toilet in the middle. These squares were known as courts. Often these houses would be 'back-to-backs'. They looked like ordinary houses from both back and front but in fact the 'back' was a separate house. Sometimes these houses simply fell down because they were so badly built.

Many houses were three storeys high, with the bottom floor having a separate door of its own to make two homes in one house. The worst houses of this type were really ordinary houses with just a cellar underneath. You had to go down steps to enter the bottom storey. These were known as 'cellar dwellings' and often it was only just possible to stand up in them. The poorest people lived in these dark, damp cellars, perhaps a whole family in just one room. In the worst part of Merthyr, a poor area known as 'China', it was said that the beds in the cellar-dwellings never got cold. They were rented to very poor workers for eight hours at a time.

Houses were often overcrowded because, although being so tiny, they often held more than one family. There was not much space left for furniture, even if people could afford it. A newspaper reporter wrote about a labourer's home in 1848:

The house consisted of two rooms and was inhabited by

two families and a lodger. In the upstairs room were three straw beds on the floor. The men and their wives occupied two of them and the children the third. There was not a table in the house; the only furniture in the downstairs room was a cradle made of a bottle case and three small benches. A teapot, a tin kettle, a can, two jugs, one candlestick and a brown pan were the only contents which this house contained. There were four ragged children who, with the women, were barefoot and dirty. One woman admitted she had buried three children; the other had lost two.

The same reporter visited a house in 'China' where the owner, a woman, was paid 5s. (25p) a week to look after two pauper children as well as three of her own. He wrote:

An old table, two chairs and a stool were the only furniture in the main room of the house. We found the children squatted round a handful of fire. The house was filthy and stinking. The eldest girl had a look of intelligence, about nine years old. Like the others she was barefoot and in rags, her hair was tangled and her face and neck were black with dirt. Here, without sheets and blankets, and with only a filthy cover, these five children passed the bitterly cold nights of winter.

DISEASE

The most terrible problem of all was not the cold or the overcrowding or the damp. It was disease. Merthyr was the unhealthiest town in the whole of Britain. More people died there of diseases than anywhere else, especially among the poor. The average life of a worker was only twenty-two years. For a member of an ironmaster family it was fifty, for a lawyer forty and for a shopkeeper it was over sixty. The average was so low among the working classes because so many young children died. In fact, three-quarters of all deaths were of children under five. The worst year of all was 1823 when, for every thousand children baptised, 713 died under the age of five. Once a child passed the age of five his chances improved. Under five, children were simply not strong enough to overcome disease.

No.	When taken ill.	When died.	Where died.	Sex.	Age.	Occupation.	Circumstances.	Habits.	Any evidence of contagion or infection.	State of the Dwellings or Neighbourhood.
1	22nd August	24th August	15, David square, Abercannaid	M.	36	Wife of Puddler (Welsh)	Very poor	Dirty	No possible contact	Damp, dirty, and unventilated.
2	22nd ,,	25th ,,	57, Quarry row, Tydfil's Well	F.	45	Wife of Fireman (Irish)	Poor	Dirty	ditto	Dirty, unventilated—yard at back most filthy.
3	23rd ,,	25th ,,	31, do do	M.	32	Fireman (Welsh)	Good	Clean and regular	ditto	A drain, which carries away house slops from houses above, runs under the house.
4	23rd ,,	26th ,,	13, Morris court, Merthyr	F.	75	Rag cleaner (Irish)	Poor	Clean	As a rag cleaner might have picked infected clothes	An untrapped gully at end of court, also heaps of ashes steeped with excrement, &c. House, no ventilation.
5	24th ,,	25th ,,	7, Cwm Canol street, Dowlais	M.	21	Hooker in Iron Mills (Irish)	Young Irish Labourer	Regular	No possible contact	Cesspool at back of house above level of lower floor—offensive.
6	24th ,,	25th ,,	1, Flag & Castle ct., Dowlais	M.	8	Son of Labourer (English)	Very poor	Dirty	ditto	Court unpaved, no convenience, earth sodden with house refuse.
7	24th ,,	1st September	16, Sunny Bank, Tydfil's Well	F.	53	Wife of Tailor (Welsh)	Very poor	Intemperate & Dirty	ditto	Cesspool in garden overflowing, floor of sleeping room thickly covered with dirt and filth.
8	25th ,,	27th August	1, Miles' court, Caedraw	F.	50	Wife of Hawker (Scotch)	Poor	Clean and regular	Her husband and herself travelled about the neighbouring towns—had been in Aberdare	Cesspool near house overflowing.
9	26th ,,	30th ,,	8, Coffin's ct., George Town	F.	80	Wife of Skinner (Welsh)	Poor	Very clean	Had attended her son, case No. 3	Unventilated—common cesspool in gardens full.
10	27th ,,	1st September	4, Lewis' square, Abercannaid	F.	32	Wife of Collier (Welsh)	Comfortable	Clean and regular	Apparently spontaneous	Overcrowded with family and lodgers—9 out of the 12 attacked, 7 died. At back of bedroom heap of ashes foul with excrement.

These details of cholera deaths in 1866 are taken from the 'Second Annual Report on the Sanitary Condition of Merthyr Tydfil'

Killer diseases came often to Merthyr. *Tuberculosis* was always present. It was a disease which spread in overcrowded, damp and dirty houses. Apart from this there were frequent outbreaks of *smallpox*, *typhoid* and measles. The worst killer of all was the dreaded *cholera* which produced terrible sickness and a swift death. This disease visited Merthyr four times between 1832 and 1866. The worst outbreak was in 1849 when over 1,300 people died. Lady Charlotte Guest wrote that in Dowlais alone there were sometimes 'over twenty people dying in one day, and eight men constantly making coffins'.

There was a simple reason for these dreadful diseases – dirt. Gradually people began to see that dirt and disease were connected, but even so those in authority did little about it. The answer was simple. It was to bring fresh, clean water to the people and to build drains and sewers to take away the filth and waste. To do this, however, would cost a great deal of money, and it was nobody's job in Merthyr to do anything about this.

It is difficult to imagine how filthy Merthyr was. In 1849 a government official, who was used to inspecting dirty industrial towns, wrote that Merthyr was the worst place he had ever seen. There were only two sewers in the whole town, and they were only a few yards long. Many of the houses had no toilets at all, and the people simply threw the contents of their chamber pots into the street or the river. Toilets, for those lucky enough to have them, were only holes in the ground that had to be regularly emptied. There were no dustbins, and the narrow streets were never cleaned. They were so littered with filth and rubbish that people had to pick their way down the middle of the road. People said in Cardiff that if a man walked along the middle of the road, he must have come from Merthyr!

There was no proper water supply. The people got their water from a few wells and springs. These would often dry up in the summer and long queues had to wait for hours to fill up their buckets and pans. They got water from the river too, but it was dirty with the waste from the ironworks and the town which drained into it.

Only in 1860 did the Merthyr Board of Health first provide

public taps for the townspeople and begin to build proper sewers to drain away the filth. Even so the number of deaths remained very high. Only the really tough survived in Merthyr.

ESCAPING FROM A HARD LIFE

Hard toil, poor food, disease, even an early death awaited most folk in those days. What could they do to make life easier?

Many people drank too much to forget their miseries. One thing that Merthyr did possess was a huge number of public houses. Men, women and even children could spend their hard-earned money on alcohol. Drinking brought disaster to many families at that time. Money that should have been spent on food was wasted on drink.

Many workers became so depressed that they decided to emigrate. This was a very difficult decision to make because it meant leaving families and friends, everything they knew, for ever. Once they had gone, there was no coming back. America was the most popular place to go to in the nineteenth century, especially the iron towns of Pennsylvania. There the Welsh ironworkers could find jobs and higher wages. Emigration became especially popular when the ironmasters sacked workers and cut wages.

Most people, however, lived out their lives in Merthyr. Many of them tried hard to change things for the better. One way was to join together and form a trade union. This was done several times but it was not very successful until the twentieth century. The ironmasters were too strong for the unions and usually managed to stamp them out.

The problem was that the workers were not good at planning things together. They did not make their plans in advance and they found it difficult to get everyone to agree on what to do. Even so there were times when life was so bad that the workers just had to do something. At these times they rose up angrily and violently against their masters and those in authority. They could not put up with their hardships any longer. You can read about the most important of these risings in the next chapters.

7 The workers are rioting!

We may be surprised that the workers in Merthyr did not rise up more often in anger and frustration. Most of them no doubt grumbled a great deal, but did nothing to try and alter their lives. They were probably proud of being tough enough to put up with their dangers and difficulties. For most of the time they respected their masters and were grateful to have a job. However, they could get angry and violent at times, especially when the ironmasters cut wages and sacked men. In 1800 and 1816 the riots were so bad that soldiers had to be sent to

Soldiers arriving to control riots in Merthyr in 1816

Merthyr to put down the workers. But the most famous rising of the Merthyr people was in 1831. For that was the year they decided they had put up with their hardships for long enough. At last the people of Merthyr were going to do something about it.

1831 was a bad year for the iron industry. No one seemed to want to buy iron any longer. All over England and Wales ironmasters were throwing hundreds of people out of work. In Merthyr only Crawshay continued to make iron he could not sell. But even he cut his wages and sacked eighty-four puddlers – all skilled men who had worked for him for years.

You know already that the ironworkers of Merthyr were very poor. And when they were out of work they were even worse off. With no work and no money they had to struggle to stay alive, borrowing the odd few pence from the shopkeepers so that they could buy food to feed their families. But this meant that many people got into debt. And as less iron was being made, the chances of the workers getting back their jobs and being able to repay their debts also grew less. To make matters worse, just when everything possible seemed to be going wrong the Court of Requests sent round its bailiffs. No one in Merthyr was safe. If you could not pay your debts with money then the bailiffs took what possessions you had.

It was even worse for the people who worked for Guest and Homfray, for they were in debt to the truck shops. No wonder the newspapers were full of articles asking for a new law which would get rid of the hated truck shops. But Parliament did not seem to take any notice. To the people of Merthyr it was clear that if they wanted to improve their lives they would have to take matters into their own hands.

In 1830 and 1831 there had been riots and meetings all over England and Wales for the reform of Parliament. Many people thought that all men, not just the rich, should have the right to vote. Only then, they said, would the people get good laws. In Merthyr some people supported these ideas. William Crawshay himself was one of the leading supporters for the reform of Parliament. In April 1831 he even encouraged some

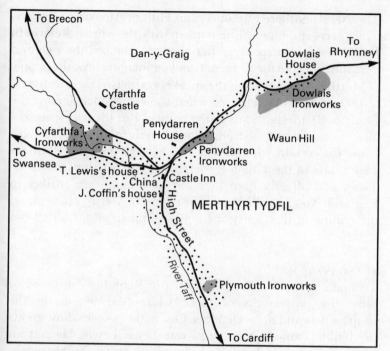

Merthyr Tydfil during the riots in 1831

of his workers to sign a petition demanding changes in Parliament. But most people in Merthyr were more concerned about their own lives. They wanted changes in Merthyr, not in Parliament. Some people, strangers from the North of England, said they should start up trade unions, go on strike and demand better wages. But that would take time and the people of Merthyr wanted action now. They had suffered for long enough and they were not going to put up with their miserable lives any longer.

For a few days in May and June 1831 they seemed to be getting their own way, but it was not to last for long.

MONDAY, 30 MAY 1831

By the end of May people were so angry that a huge meeting was arranged so that they could protest about their complaints. 45

Thousands gathered up on Waun Hill, overlooking Merthyr. They carried a huge white banner with the words 'Reform in Parliament', and speaker after speaker attacked the rich and demanded a vote for all men. Can you imagine how the people of Merthyr clapped when the speakers criticised their ironmasters? And how they cheered when someone spoke against the Court of Requests and its hated bailiffs? But the best speech of all came at the end. A stranger stood on the platform. We don't know for certain who he was but he was probably William Twiss, one of the Union leaders from the North of England. Twiss had already been involved in a number of strikes in England. Now he called upon the people of Merthyr to demand the ending of the Court of Requests and to go for an all-out strike.

TUESDAY, 31 MAY 1831

To make matters worse, the Court of Requests continued to seize the possessions of those who owed money to the shopkeepers and moneylenders. One of the people whose goods the bailiffs came to take away was Lewis Lewis. He was an ironstone miner, a hard worker, well-respected by his neighbours. Everyone called him Lewis the Huntsman (Lewsyn yr Heliwr) because he knew all there was to know about dogs and horses. Only the previous week the bailiffs had taken from his home a fine, oak chest. This time they were not so successful, because when they tried to break into his house, Lewis Lewis and his neighbours crowded round and chased the bailiffs off. Even more daring, the neighbours planned to get back his old oak chest. Trouble was brewing...

WEDNESDAY, 1 JUNE 1831

At last the ordinary people were beginning to take action to improve their own lives and to make changes in Merthyr. They were angry about so many things but it was the Court of Requests that they hated most of all. They felt very strongly that it was unfair for the court to sell off their goods cheaply to anyone who could afford them. That day Lewis the Huntsman,

46

with a band of his friends and neighbours, seized back his oak chest. Lewis climbed on top of it and gave a fiery speech to the crowd. Historians are not sure what he said but he seemed to be planning to do the same sort of thing on the following day. Lewis was a born leader of men, and there were plenty of volunteers to get back the possessions that the bailiffs had taken away from the people. In those excitable days of 1831 people did not need much to encourage them. That very evening some of them – no-one knows who – threw *fireballs* through the windows of the house of Joseph Coffin, the President of the Court of Requests.

THURSDAY, 2 JUNE 1831

During the morning gangs of angry workers roamed through the town, visiting the homes of those who bought goods taken by the Court of Requests. They asked for them back – clocks, watches, furniture, even Bibles – and returned them to the original owners. If anyone refused, the people went into their homes and took the goods anyway.

In the afternoon the gangs joined up into a great crowd. They took their orders from their leaders, Lewis the Huntsman and his two friends Dai Soloman and Dai Iron-hand. They decided to visit the homes of two men who were particularly hated by the people of Merthyr. Thomas Williams, the nastiest of the bailiffs, was one of these. The other was Thomas Lewis, a moneylender.

By the time the crowd reached Thomas Lewis's house, it was in an ugly mood. Some people wanted to beat up Thomas Lewis and even threatened to kill him. One man threw him to the ground and another knocked his wife on top of him. Fortunately for Thomas Lewis two *magistrates* arrived on the scene. One was the Chief Magistrate, Mr. Bruce, who was in charge of law and order in Merthyr. The other was Anthony Hill, the ironmaster. They tried to break up the crowd but no-one would listen to them.

The leaders of the crowd now decided to go even further against the law and to get all the people on their side. They sent

47

messengers to all four ironworks to stop the furnaces. and to bring out the workers. Meanwhile, some of the crowd marched off to Joseph Coffin's house to destroy the account books in which all the people's debts were written down. Coffin tried to fool them by handing over some old account books but this made them even more enraged, especially the rougher members of the crowd. One of the constables, John Thomas, bravely but foolishly stood up to them. He might even have been killed if Lewis the Huntsman had not saved him. Lewis threw himself across John Thomas' body as it was being beaten and kicked. He shouted loudly that he would allow no murder. Instead the crowd swarmed into Joseph Coffin's house and burned his furniture in the street. At last they found the real account books and tore them into shreds. No more debts now.

At this stage the people in authority could do little against the rioters as they had no troops and only a few constables. However Mr. Bruce did set up his special headquarters in the Castle Inn on High Street (in the picture below). That evening William Crawshay and Josiah John Guest, the chief ironmasters, returned to Merthyr from business elsewhere. As soon as they arrived it was decided to send messages to Cardiff and Brecon to call for soldiers. But the people of Merthyr were expecting this and were making plans to deal with it.

The Castle Inn in Merthyr High Street, drawn in 1841

8 The rising fails

FRIDAY, 3 JUNE 1831

This was the saddest and most dangerous day of the Rising. It began well for the people of Merthyr, but by nightfall they were swearing vengeance on the ironmasters and magistrates in authority over them.

Some of the workers had spent the whole of the previous night shutting down all the furnaces in Merthyr. By early morning a large crowd was gathering in the market place and soon there were thousands of people shouting and marching all around the town. This time they had a red flag, the flag of revolution, not a white one. There was a loaf of bread stuck on its point.

At ten o'clock came the news that soldiers were arriving. These soldiers had set out from Brecon as soon as the messengers had arrived the night before. Angrily the crowd rushed up to the Brecon road to meet them. Some of the rioters wanted to bar their way but this was too risky, for even though there were only eighty soldiers they were all well-armed. Clubs, iron bars and sticks were no match for the soldiers' *muskets*. Instead the people jeered and mocked the soldiers. The government in those days did not use local troops to put down a riot in case they sided with the rioters. So these soldiers were Highlanders, dressed in their kilts. 'Women, you can't beat us', chanted the crowd.

The soldiers marched straight to the Castle Inn, where they lined up in front of the building. There was a lot of punching and shoving as the excited crowd pushed up against them. Lewis Lewis and the other leaders were there, watching and

49

standing by the red banner. Some of the ironmasters tried to speak but were howled down. At last Lewis and his friends went inside the inn to talk to the Chief Magistrate Mr. Bruce and the ironmasters. One of these workers was Richard Lewis who was better known by his nickname, Dic Penderyn. He was a tough young man, a miner well-known in the town as a hard fighter. Of course no agreement was reached inside the inn, and, when the workers came outside to report that they had had no success, a frightening roar of anger arose from the whole crowd.

Suddenly things became very dangerous indeed. Bruce shouted to the people to go home, threatening to order the soldiers to fire on them. Several of the younger men squeezed between the soldiers and the inn wall, surrounding and squashing them so tight that they could not raise their muskets. The rest of the crowd called for Josiah John Guest to grant their demands. They preferred him to the hated Crawshay. Both masters spoke to their workers from the upstairs windows of the inn, but Crawshay only enraged the crowd even more by shouting down that he would not listen to them. The crowd was really angry now.

Then Lewis Lewis gave the order that his followers had been waiting for. 'Boys, take their guns away, off with their guns!' It was impossible to know what was really happening. There was some very fierce and nasty fighting. The rioters forced some of the soldiers to leave go of their guns, but others managed to stab out with the *bayonets* which were fixed to the end of their muskets. There was blood everywhere. Some men were already dead, others were moaning and holding their wounds. Time after time the mob rushed into the passageway of the inn, but every time they were pushed back by the soldiers inside.

Then came the terrible order from inside the inn, 'Fire, men, fire!' At once some soldiers in the upstairs rooms started shooting at the unarmed crowd. The people down below just stopped still in surprise for a moment. Then there was panic. Many rioters ran away as fast as they could, and even as they ran the soldiers shot them in the back. Others however stayed to fight back with captured muskets, with sticks and stones and with their bare fists. In the end they were forced off the street but Lewis the Huntsman continued to lead charge after charge through the stable yard at the back of the inn. He could be heard shouting, 'Stand your ground, stand your ground, lads!'

But the soldiers had many weapons and the workers had very few. The day ended in defeat for the rioters. Sixteen people were killed that day, three women and a young boy among them. More died of their injuries in the next few days and others nursed their wounds in secret, afraid to call for the doctors in case their guilt became known. But the defeat was not final. The ironmasters and the magistrates decided that the Castle Inn was too dangerous for them. They moved their headquarters to Penydarren House just outside the town. More troops arrived from Cardiff and Newport but only the eighty Highlanders from Brecon were full-time soldiers. Anthony Hill was sent galloping off to Cardiff for more full-time troops.

The rioters, too, made their preparations. Lewis Lewis and the other leaders began to collect proper weapons for the next battle. They sent a message to Hirwaun, Aberdare and to other neighbouring iron towns, 'We need your help. We workers must stand together'. The troubles in Merthyr were certainly not yet over.

SATURDAY, 4 JUNE 1831

At the beginning of the day the result of the rising was still undecided. Victories were won during the day by both sides. Only if the workers could increase their support and stick together could they win, yet the masters were already hard at work trying to split them up.

The people of Hirwaun and Aberdare supported the workers of Merthyr. It was said that they even sacrificed a calf and soaked their flag in its blood. They marched behind it that morning to join the rising in Merthyr. In Merthyr itself more men and women joined the fight, sickened by the slaughter of the previous day. Lewis Lewis set up his own headquarters on the high, barren hillside of Dan-y-Graig, overlooking the 51

The Hirwaun workers bathe their flag in calf's blood. This picture was drawn by someone who was against the workers' cause

masters' base at Penydarren House. They now had nearly four hundred guns and several swords and *pitchforks*.

The rioters now acted with determination, even against armed troops. Early in the day they forced back a mule train loaded with ammunition from Brecon. The authorities sent a hundred troops from Penydarren House to help it through, but the workers rolled rocks down on them from the steep sides of the road and forced them back. In the afternoon the rioters had an even greater success. A group of over thirty soldiers from Swansea was marching through the slag-heaps towards Penydarren House. Suddenly they saw the figure of a boy waving to them as if he were a friend. Foolishly they walked towards him. It was a trap. The soldiers were ambushed by a band of workers who took all their weapons off them and sent them packing back to Swansea in disgrace.

Yet on the wild hillside at Dan-y-Graig the leaders of the rising were having difficulties. They realised how important it

was to keep the workers together, but this was proving

impossible to do. Some workers wanted to make lots of changes in Merthyr, hoping that people all over the country would follow their example. A few of the more violent followers wanted to wipe out the masters and the shopkeepers altogether. Others wanted to come to an agreement with the masters, feeling that the riots and the violence had gone far enough.

This was exactly what the authorities wanted. They realised that their best plan was to split up the workers by winning over those who wanted to come to an agreement with them. From Penydarren House they issued a *proclamation*, blaming Lewis Lewis for everything that had happened outside the Castle Inn. They signed it, 'Your friends and masters'. They invited a group of workers to go and meet them, saying that they could be depended on to put things right. Some men did go to Penydarren House but the majority of rioters could not be persuaded so easily to give in. Their leaders decided to march on Penydarren House. Thousands set off but none of them arrived. They were met on the way by the men coming back from Penydarren House, who told them that the masters had promised not to reduce their wages.

Historians cannot be certain what happened next, but it seems that there was a terrible argument between those who wanted to march on, and the majority, who probably feared more terrible bloodshed and said they were satisfied with the masters' promises. In other words, the workers were split. The most the leaders could do was to decide to hold a mass meeting on Waun Hill on the following Monday. They were still hoping that the workers fom Blaenavon, Rhymney and the other iron towns would come to their aid.

SUNDAY, 5 JUNE 1831

At Penydarren House more and more troops arrived all day long, but little is known of what happened on the workers' side. On the hillside at Dan-y-Graig they practised with their weapons. Only a few supporters arrived from the other towns, but bands of men and boys were sent out to get more help for the following day.

MONDAY, 6 JUNE 1831

At last the people of the other towns arrived and the Merthyr crowd went out to meet them at Dowlais. Some said there were 20,000 people there altogether. Yet they achieved nothing at all, because the masters and the soldiers were there too to stop the newcomers from marching into the town. At first Crawshay and Guest tried unsuccessfully to stop the crowd with speeches. Only when the soldiers moved forward with their muskets loaded and their bayonets pointing towards the people did the crowd begin to split up. The new arrivals went straight back to their own towns while the Merthyr people went to their headquarters at Dan-y-Graig. It is difficult for historians to know what happened there but it seems that everyone was shouting and arguing about what to do. Some wanted to go ahead with the planned meeting at Waun Hill, while others wanted to go back to work.

By the middle of the afternoon the rising was finished. The disheartened people hid or threw away the weapons they had so carefully collected and made their way home in defeat. They could only wait now to see what the authorities would do to them.

TUESDAY, 7 JUNE 1831

All day the manhunt went on. Soldiers marched round the streets for hours to frighten the people. Workers who still had a job returned to the ironworks to start up the furnaces under the suspicious eyes of the masters. One by one the leaders of the rising were arrested. One of the last to be captured was Lewis the Huntsman. He put up a good fight when the troops at last caught up with him in the woods.

FRIDAY, 8 JUNE 1831

The prisoners were marched off to Cardiff Gaol to stand trial. They were tied up like slaves with iron chains round their necks and feet. It was Crawshay who provided the chains and the prisoners' own workmates who made them. The riots were well and truly over.

9 The legend of Dic Penderyn

The rising may have been defeated but the people had not yet
been really crushed. They had learned a lesson: they now knew
that it was no use simply rioting and expecting the masters to
give in. Even more important, they realised that they had not
been united enough against the authorities. They vowed that
next time they would make better preparations and would act
together.

The best way to achieve this seemed to be through a union.
Already the union leaders from the North of England were
busily helping them to form a union. Only if this was done in
secret could the union hope to grow, or else the masters would
destroy it. The workers therefore swore their oaths of loyalty to
the union behind closed doors and promised never to give away
its secrets. There were plenty of volunteers in those days
following the rising, even though if a man was suspected of
joining a union he was immediately dismissed from work.

Meanwhile the leaders of the rioting were still awaiting trial
in Cardiff.

THURSDAY, 14 JULY 1831

Merthyr was in a fury. The trial of twenty-eight rioters had
started the day before. It had been expected to go on for several
days but the judge suddenly decided to stop it on the second
day and to release most of the prisoners. Only six men were
found guilty. Four were sentenced to *transportation*, to be sent
away for life to the prison settlements in Australia. Their crime
was entering the home of Thomas Lewis the moneylender on 2
55

June. This was a severe punishment, even for those days, and it shocked the people of Merthyr. But what were more shocking were the sentences given to Lewis Lewis and Dic Penderyn. Both were sentenced to death by public hanging. Lewis Lewis was found guilty of ordering the crowd to take the guns off the soldiers outside the Castle Inn on 3 June. Dic Penderyn was sentenced for stabbing one of the soldiers, Donald Black, in the leg on the same occasion.

The people of Merthyr were probably not really surprised that Lewis the Huntsman was to be severely punished. After all he was the main leader of the rising. What they could not really understand was the death sentence on Dic Penderyn. He did not really play a very important part in the rising and he was only condemned on the evidence of one man, James Abbott, who swore that he saw Dic stick a bayonet into Donald Black's leg. It seems that it was well known in Merthyr that James Abbott, a local barber, had been swearing to get his revenge on Dic Penderyn ever since they had had a fight a few months earlier.

It has never been made clear why the judge stopped the trial so suddenly, releasing so many of the accused. He probably wanted to make an example of the two sentenced men.

THURSDAY, 28 JULY 1831

Ever since the trial the inhabitants of Merthyr had been gathering a huge *petition* of signatures, begging the government to stop the death sentences. Now came the news that it had been turned down. The only remaining hope of the accused men lay in the attempts of a man called Joseph Price to get them released. He was an ironmaster whose works were at Neath a few miles from Merthyr. He was a member of the Quaker religion who had a very strong sense of justice and who took up the cause of Lewis Lewis and Dic Penderyn because he felt they had been very unjustly treated. He travelled to London to plead with Lord Melbourne, the Home Secretary, who had the power to pardon the two men. Joseph Price stated that, after all, Lewis Lewis had deliberately saved the life of the police constable on the night when the crowd attacked Joseph Coffin's house, proving that he was not really an evil man. As for Dic Penderyn, Joseph Price had found many witnesses to swear that Dic was not in front of the Castle Inn at the time the soldier was stabbed. So, even though the petition had been turned down, there was good reason to expect that the two men would be spared.

SUNDAY, 31 JULY 1831

The good news arrived that Lewis the Huntsman's death sentence had been set aside and that, instead, he would be transported to Australia for life. It was a terrible punishment, but at least he would not die. Dic Penderyn's sentence too was postponed for a few days to give Joseph Price time to find more evidence. The people of Merthyr felt more hopeful at last.

WEDNESDAY, 10 AUGUST 1831

The final terrible news arrived from London. Lord Melbourne had turned down all Joseph Price's new evidence. More and more witnesses had come forward to declare that the man who stabbed the soldier was one of those who had later been killed outside the Castle Inn. Some swore that James Abbott the barber was inside the inn at the time and therefore could not have seen the stabbing. No one in Merthyr believed that Dic was guilty, not even the ironmasters. William Crawshay himself sent money to pay for Dic's lawyers. But now there was no chance of a reprieve. Dic was to die as an example to any would-be rioters that the government would deal firmly with them.

SATURDAY, 13 AUGUST 1831

Hundreds of Merthyr people walked to Cardiff to watch Dic die. They wanted to be near him in his few final moments. Dic's wife was there, his family, his comrades. Their hearts were with him but they could do nothing, they were helpless. There were curious by-standers, too, watching the execution outside the gaol in busy St Mary's Street. How humiliating to die in public, 57 how shaming to be hanged before the gaze of thousands. Dic died quickly. The hangman pulled on his legs to make the rope tighten more surely round his neck.

Dic was not a particularly good man. He drank too much, and fought a lot. But he was a brave man and, more importantly, he was an innocent man. Right to the end he declared his innocence. He shouted to the crowds that he was not a murderer, that he had done no worse than hundreds of others. He died courageously, but his last words on the scaffold in Cardiff have never been forgotten: 'Oh Lord, what injustice!'

SUNDAY, 14 AUGUST 1831

Dic was buried in the afternoon, but not in Merthyr because the magistrates would not allow his funeral for fear of riots. His body had to go back to its birthplace at Aberafon along the coast. A great procession accompanied it for hours on its journey from Cardiff. It was a sad and angry crowd that followed the farmcart carrying Dic's body through the country lanes of Glamorgan. The preacher had to stand on the churchyard wall so that the hundreds of mourners could hear the service of burial. There was a long, sad silence as Dic's body was lowered into the grave. Dic at last was at rest, but the people of Merthyr were all thinking the same thought: 'O Lord, what injustice!'

A modern gravestone in memory of Dic Penderyn

Things To Do

1. Imagine that you are an ironmaster and you are going to bring in one of the new inventions. Write a speech which you will make to your workforce, giving your reasons for using the new invention.
2. Make a time-chart, showing the main events of Merthyr's history between 1748 and 1870.
3. Imagine that you work in a mine or ironworks in Merthyr. Explain the reasons and difficulties of starting a union to one of your friends who is against the idea.
4. Try to visit the National Museum of Wales in Cardiff or Merthyr's museum at Cyfarthfa Castle to find out about ironmaking and coalmining and the life of the people.
5. Write out a daily timetable of your own life nowadays. By the side of it write out the daily timetable of a boy or girl in Merthyr in 1840. Include your work, your home, your family, your meals etc.
6. Write a short play or discussion between an ironmaster's child and a pauper child.
7. Imagine that you are a worker present at the great meeting at Waun Hill on 30 May 1831. Make a list of things that you want changed.
8. Make a poster or wallchart showing the events of the Merthyr rising.
9. Draw a map of Merthyr at the time of the rising of 1831. Mark on it the dates and events of the rising. Use a map key if you need to.
10. Write a short account for an encyclopaedia of Dic Penderyn's life and death.

Glossary

adits, tunnels in the hillside from which coal is dug

bailiffs, officials from the Court of Requests who collected debts or possessions

bayonet, dagger attached to the end of a rifle

blast engine, machine to blow cold air through a furnace to heat it up more quickly

Board of Guardians, group of people who collected the poor rate and used the money to help the poor

cast iron, a fairly pure but not very strong iron

charcoal, black remains of partly burnt wood, used for fuel

cholera, highly dangerous and infectious disease, passed on by infected food or water

compensation, money paid to a worker injured in an accident

contractor, man in charge of a team of workers

Court of Requests, court where shopkeepers and money lenders collected debts from workers

fireball, ball of material which easily catches fire

founders, workers who let liquid iron out of the furnace and into the moulds

foundry, building where iron is made in furnaces

hot blast, hot air blown into the furnace by a machine to make the fire hotter

impurities, bits in iron which are not pure

ironmasters, rich owners of ironworks

locks, sections of a canal where boats can be raised or lowered between two gates

magistrate, unpaid part-time judge in a small local court

musket, an old-fashioned type of rifle

overman, leader of a team of labourers

paupers, very poor people, receiving help from the Board of Guardians

petition, list of several signatures asking an authority for something *pig iron*, iron which cools in a channel shaped like a sow feeding her piglets

pitchfork, long-handled fork with sharp prongs for lifting hay

Poor Law, law organising the treatment of poor people

poor rate, money paid by ratepayers to support the poor

proclamation, a public announcement

puddling, removing impurities from iron by stirring when reheated

ratepayers, better-off people who paid a poor rate

slag, waste material left behind by iron making

smallpox, severe disease often causing death

steel, a strong metal made by combining iron with carbon

tuberculosis, a serious and highly infectious disease

transportation, punishing a criminal by shipping him to a prisoners' community overseas

truck shop, shops owned by employers where workers had to buy their goods

typhoid, infectious disease caused by impure food or water

workhouse, building where the very poor had to live

wrought iron, strong, pure iron made by reheating and hammering cast iron

Index